Rude Girl

Chef

Cup Winner

Skateboarder

Boxing Kangaroo

Caveman

Bendy Girl

Gangster

Wise owl

Hippo Ballerina

Penguin Waiter   # Sneaky Snake

Footballer

Clown

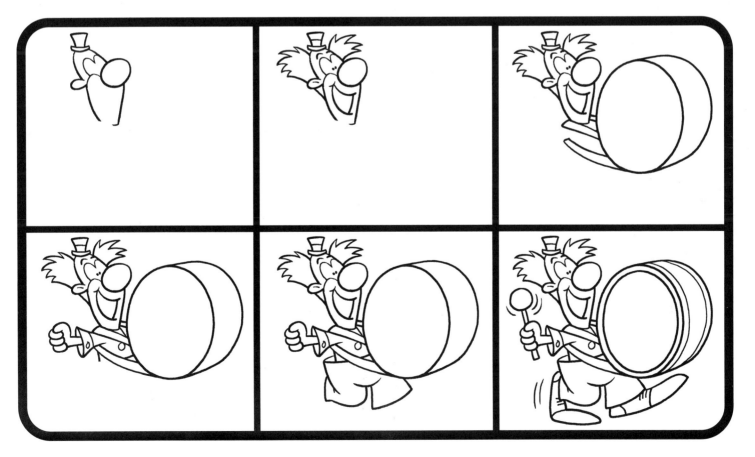

cycling Gorilla   Dancing Pharaoh

Sweeping Girl

Cool Cat

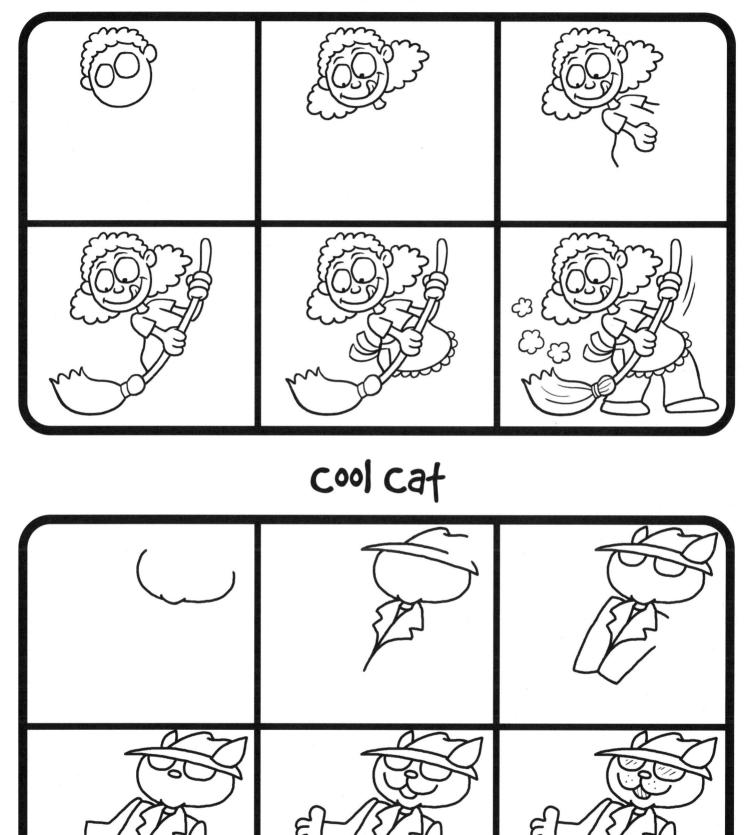

Hula Girl

Big Builder

Angry Man

Daft Dog

Karate Girl

Scarecrow

Artist

Canoeing Moose

Tourist

Parachuting

Dinghy Ride

Dinner Bear

Screaming Girl

Tarzan the Tiger

Diver

Wet Dog

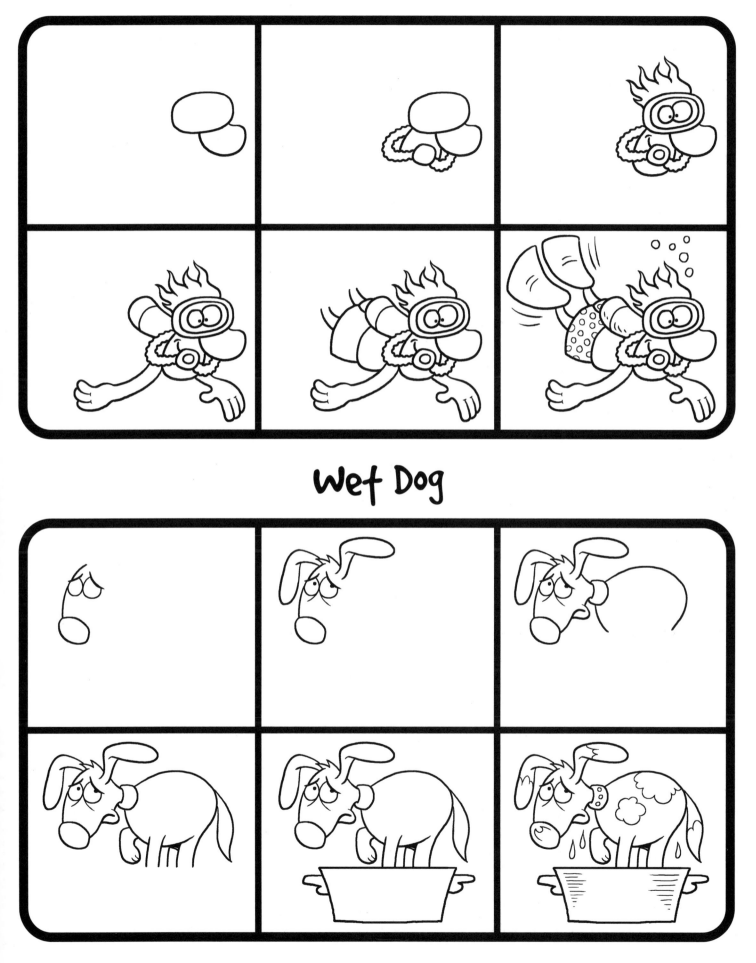

Deep Sea Diver   # Party Girl

Easter Bunny

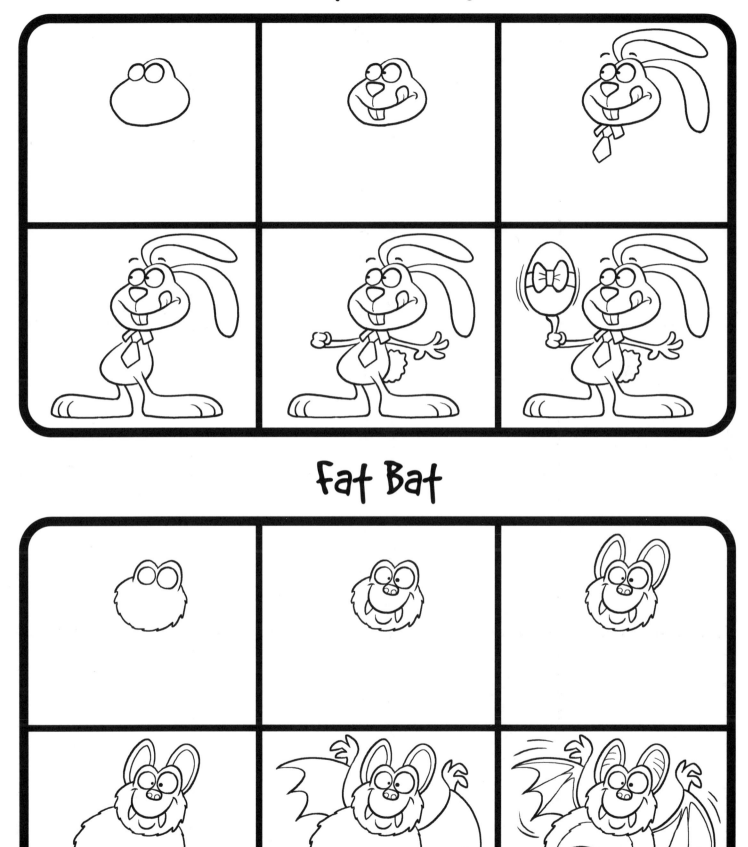

Fat Bat

Snowman

Idea boy

Ghost

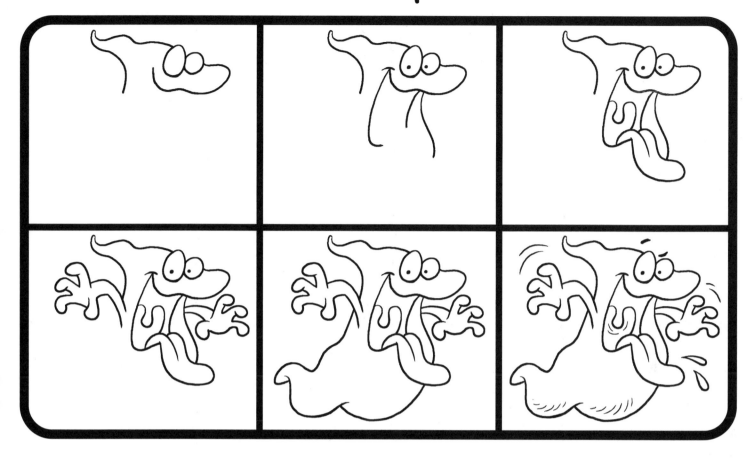

Flying Pig

Princess

Soccer Player

fisherman

Ice-hockey Player

Thin Weightlifter

Jester

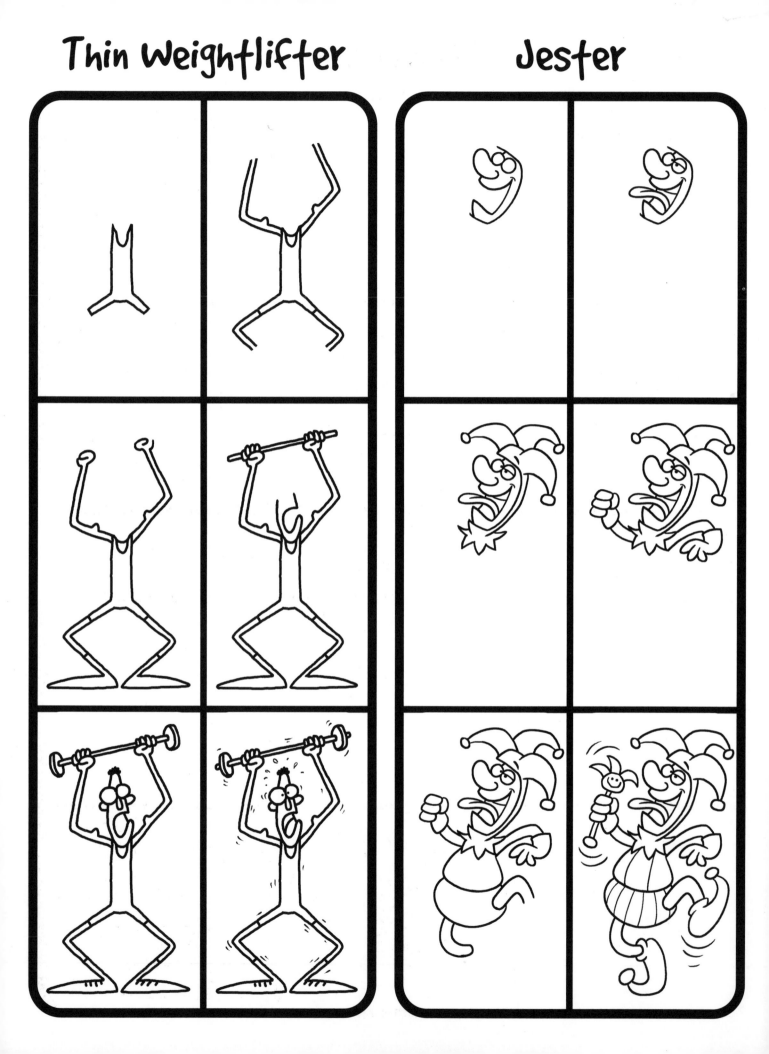

Kite Flying

Rhino on a Bike

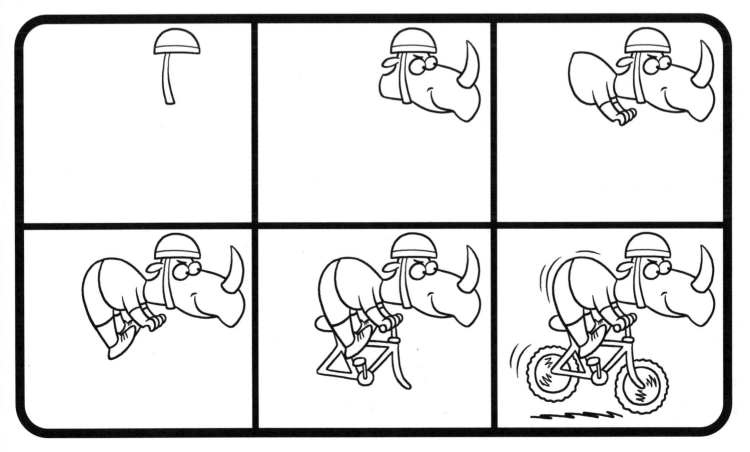

Shy Girl   Surgeon

Body Builder

old Man

Freezing

Yo-yo Boy

Skating Bear

Reindeer

Crying Baby   Duck Spy

Knight on Horseback

Rock Drummer

Hiker

Hippity Hop Girl

Teddy cuddle

Elephant Tightrope

Hungry Cat   Basketball Player

Surfing Shark

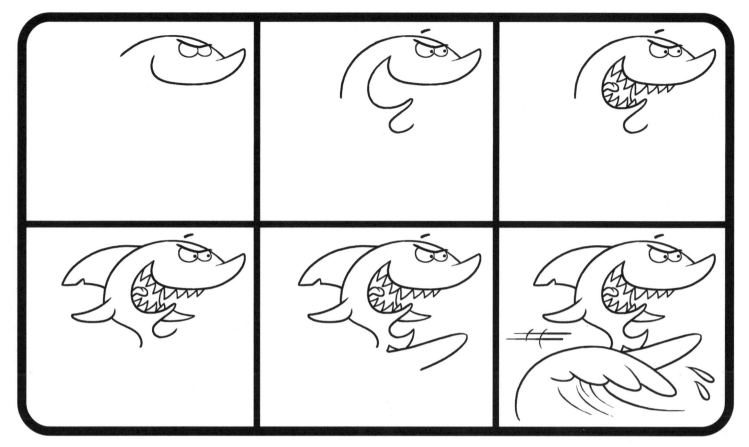

Speedy Snail

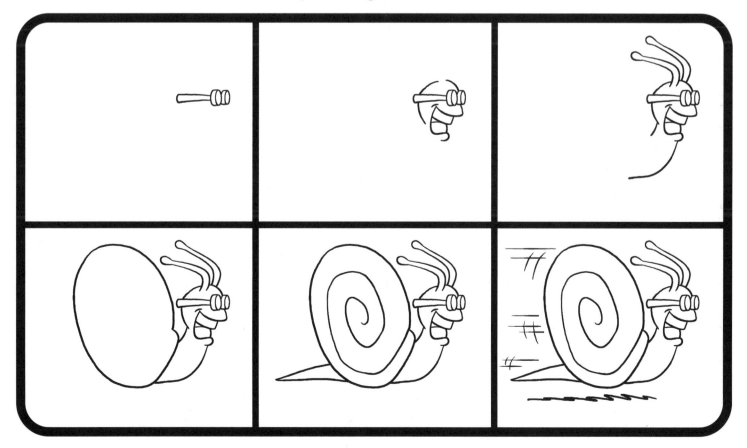

Keep-fit ostrich

Painter

Frog Swimmer

Rock Star

Boy Scout   Pirate

computer and Mouse

Tortoise

cowboy

In Love

Viking

Wizard

Scientist

Witch

Goldfish Rave

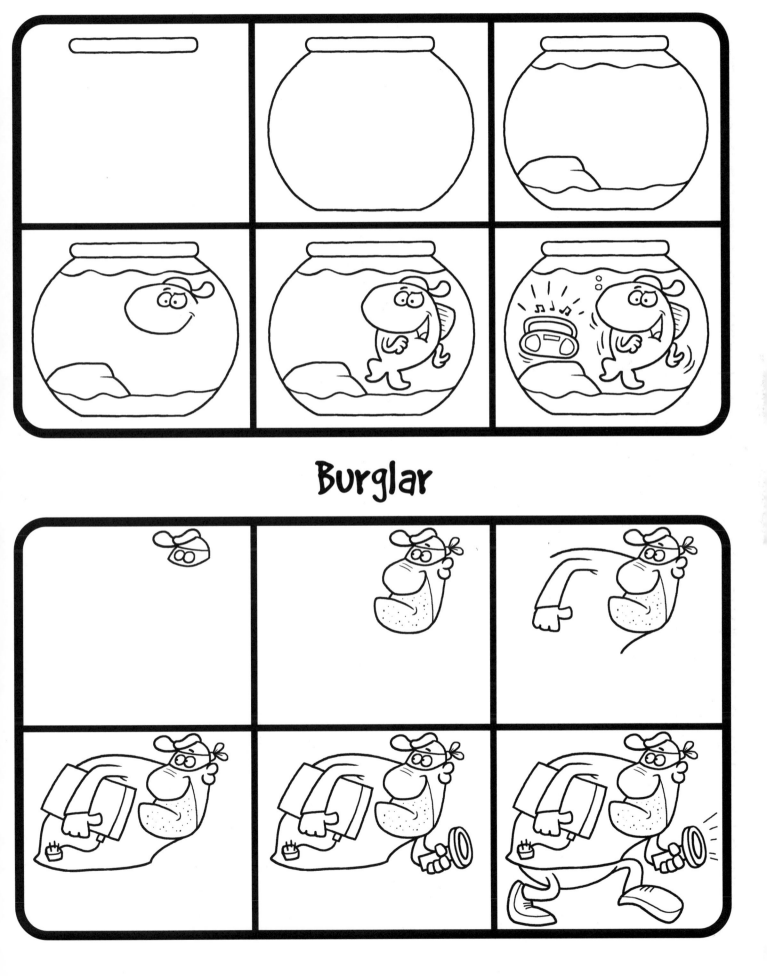

Burglar

Santa

Cheeky Chicken

Champion

Little Angel

Little Devil

Busy Beaver

Queen

Punky Parrot

Bookworm

Sheila Sheep

Cool Banana

Silly Spider

Mobile Phone

Hippy Hamster

Sherlock Bones

Lion

Pig

Lobster

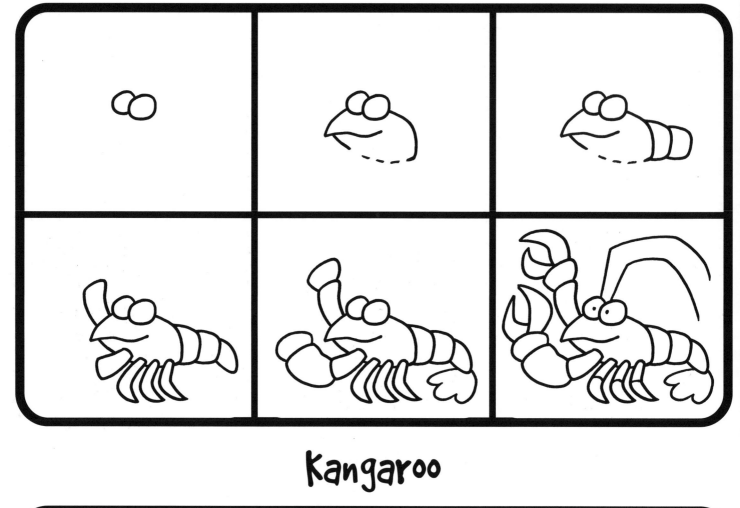

Kangaroo

Eagle

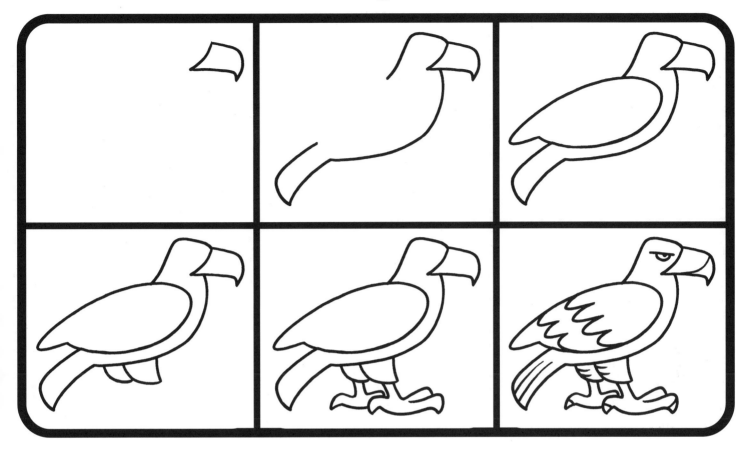

Chimpanzee

Cat

Turtle

Dog

Baboon

Fish

Tiger

Hedgehog

Kiwi

Parrot

Stag Beetle

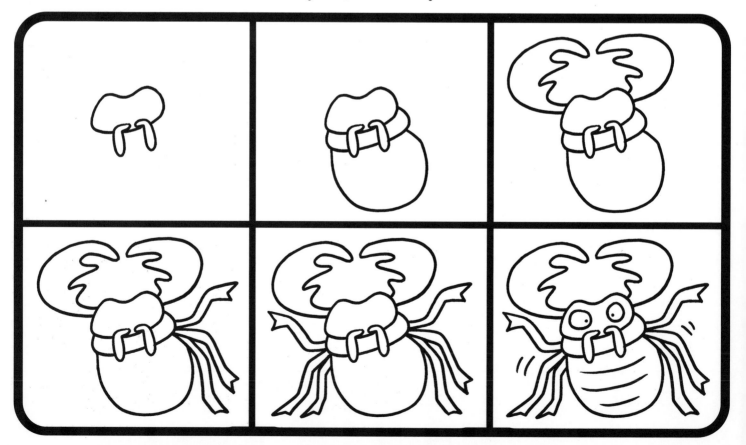

Anteater

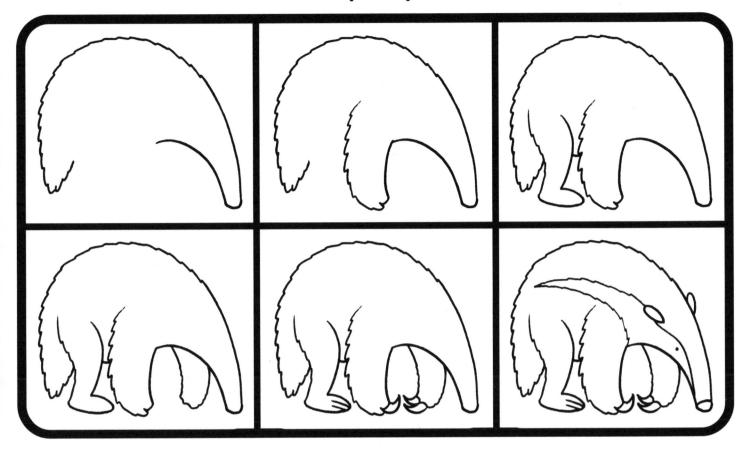

chicken

Budgie

orang-utan

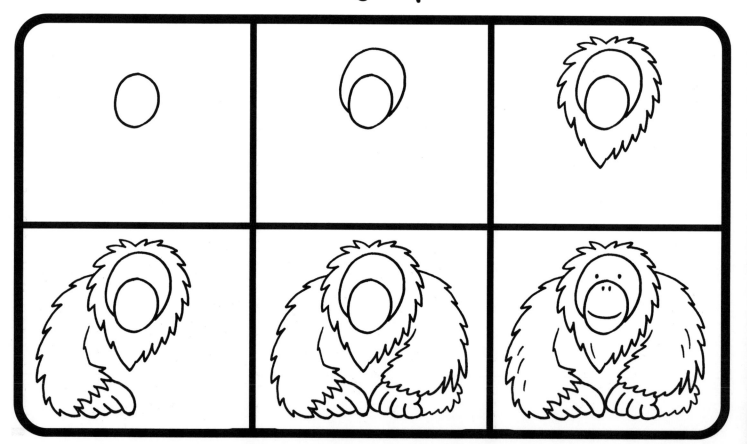

Rhino

Bat

Squirrel

Donkey

Toad

owl

crab

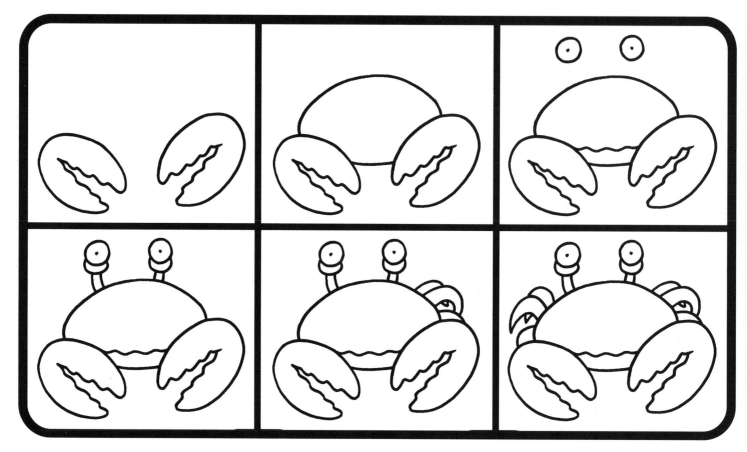

Dolphin

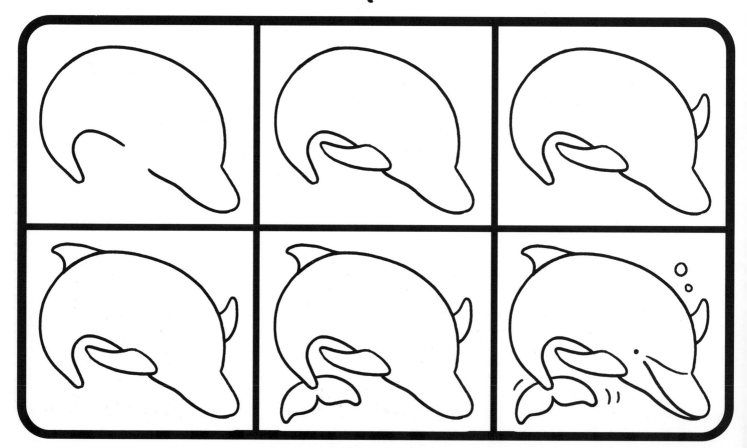

cow

Rat

Seal

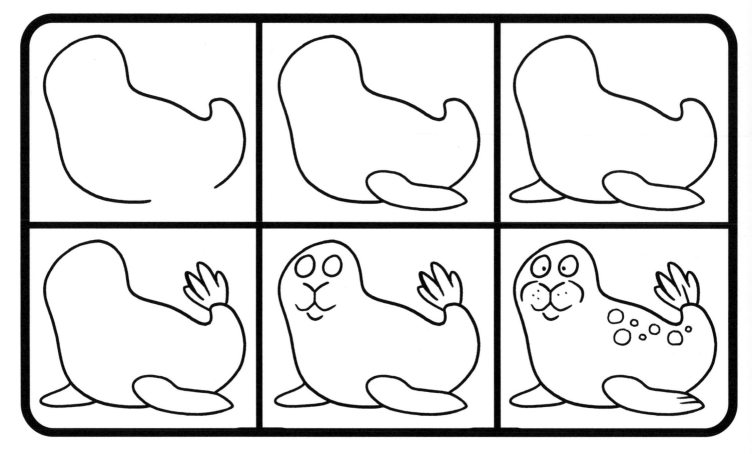

Tortoise

camel

Ant

Peacock

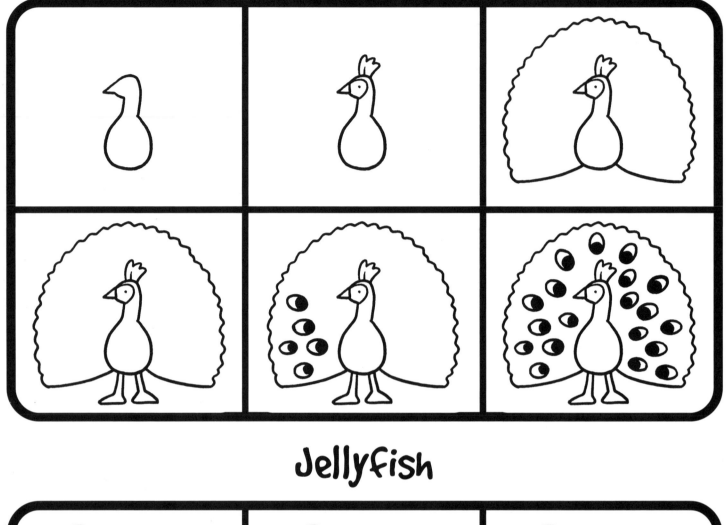

Jellyfish

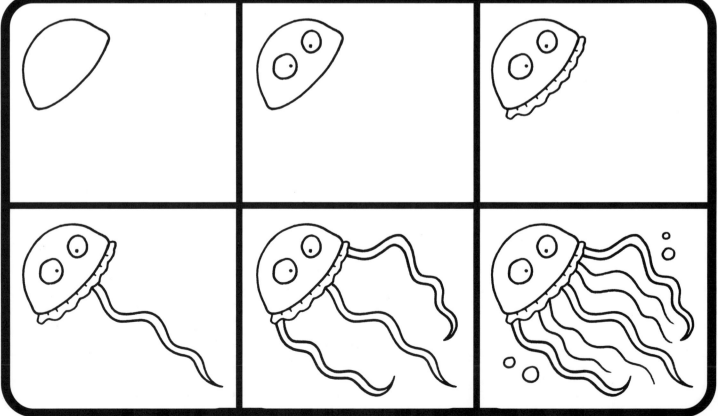

otter

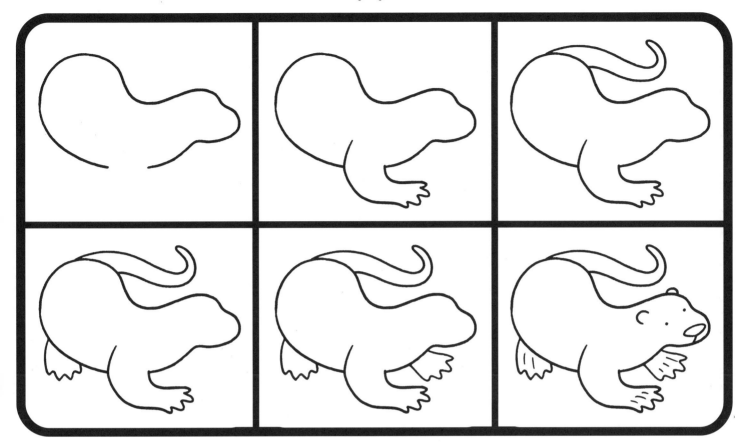

Zebra

Snail

Chameleon

Rabbit

Sheep

Panda

Snake

Killer Whale

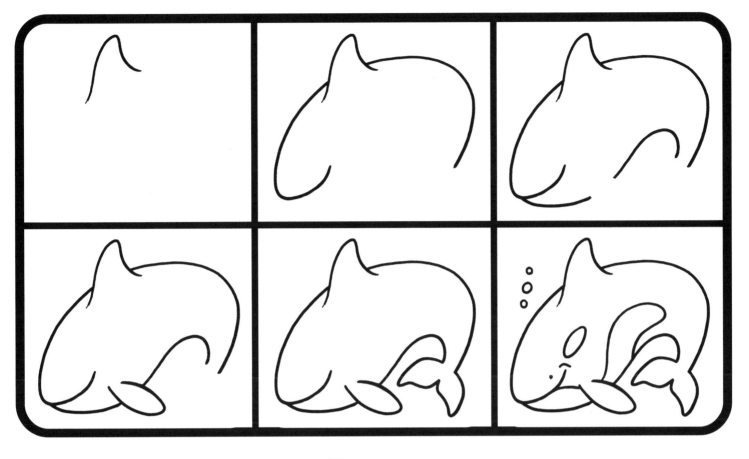

Toucan

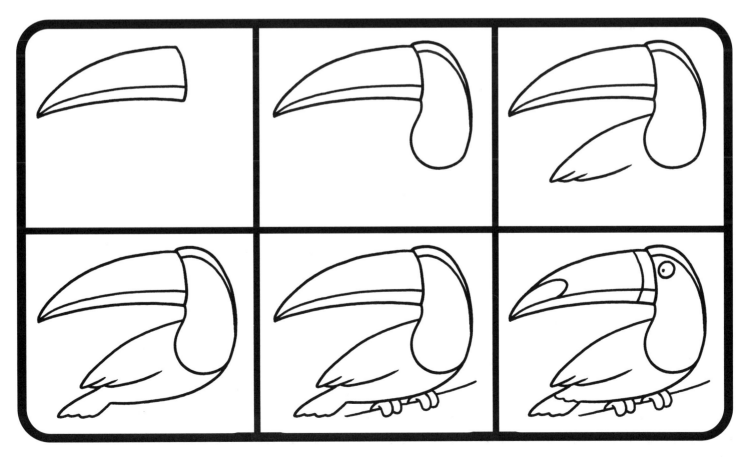

Lemur

Bison

Horse

Penguin

Elephant

Frog

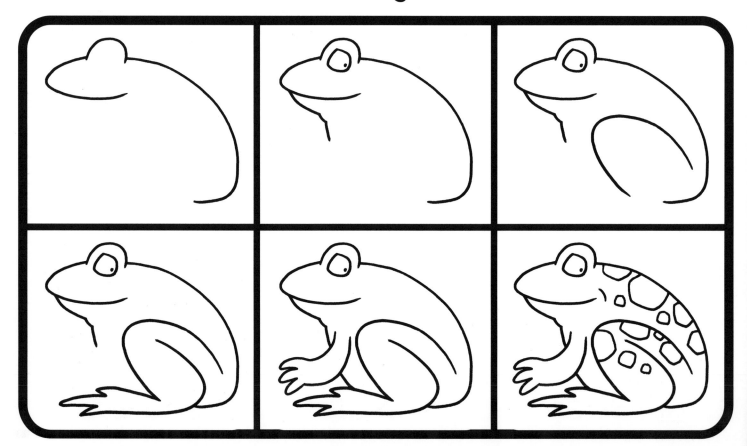

Shark

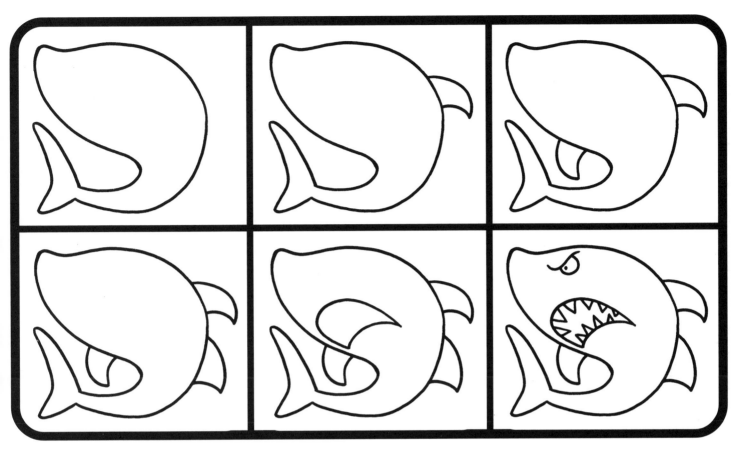

Goat

Panther

Kingfisher

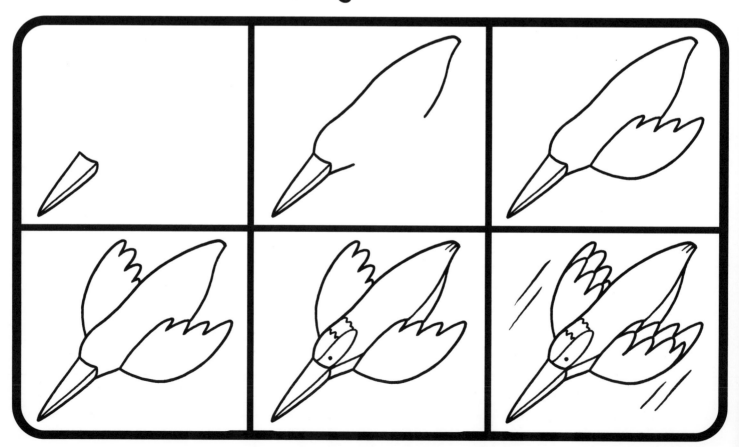

Grasshopper

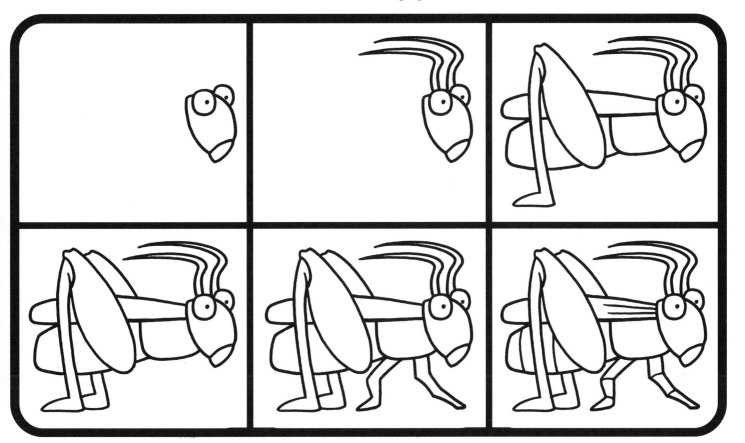

Squid

Duck

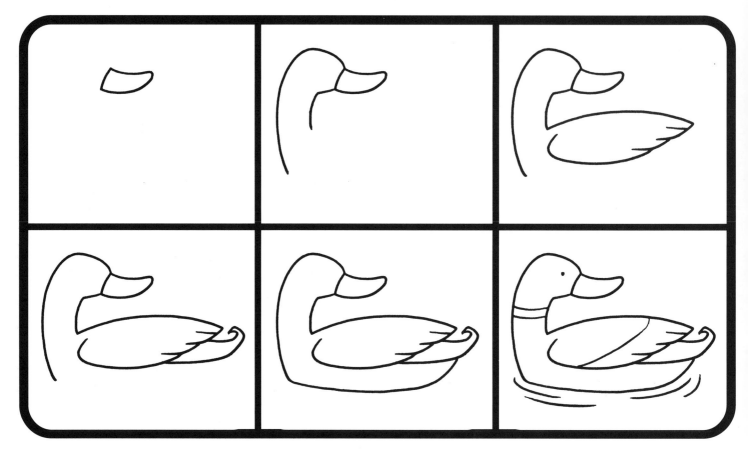

Porcupine

Humpback Whale

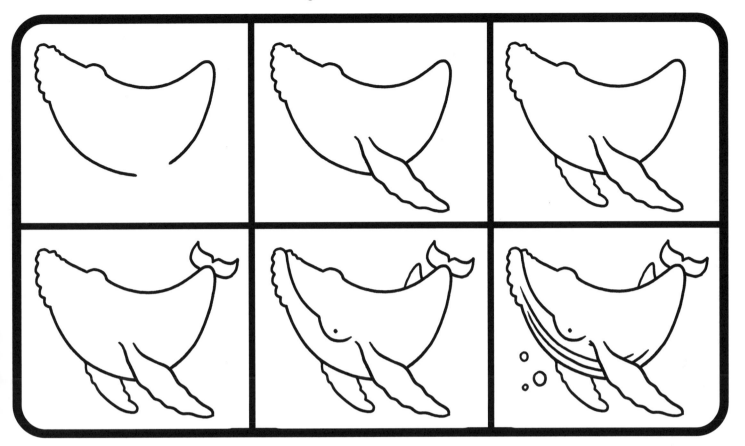

Beaver

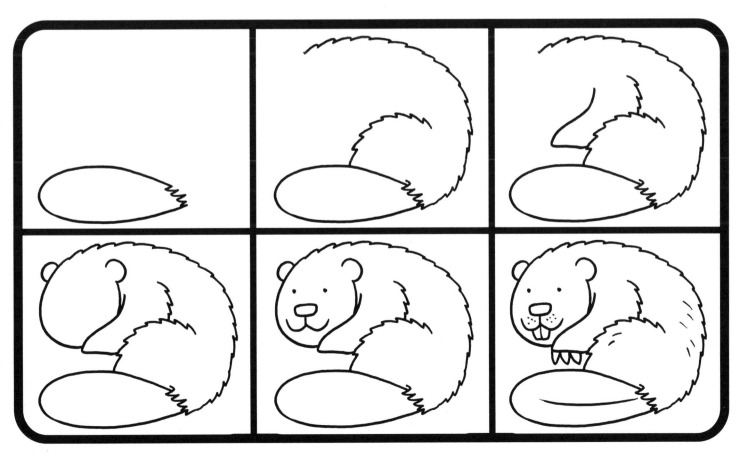

Koala

Walrus

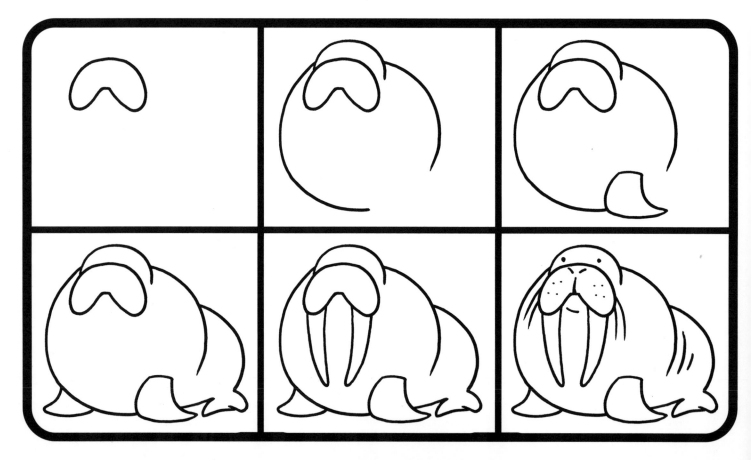

Spider

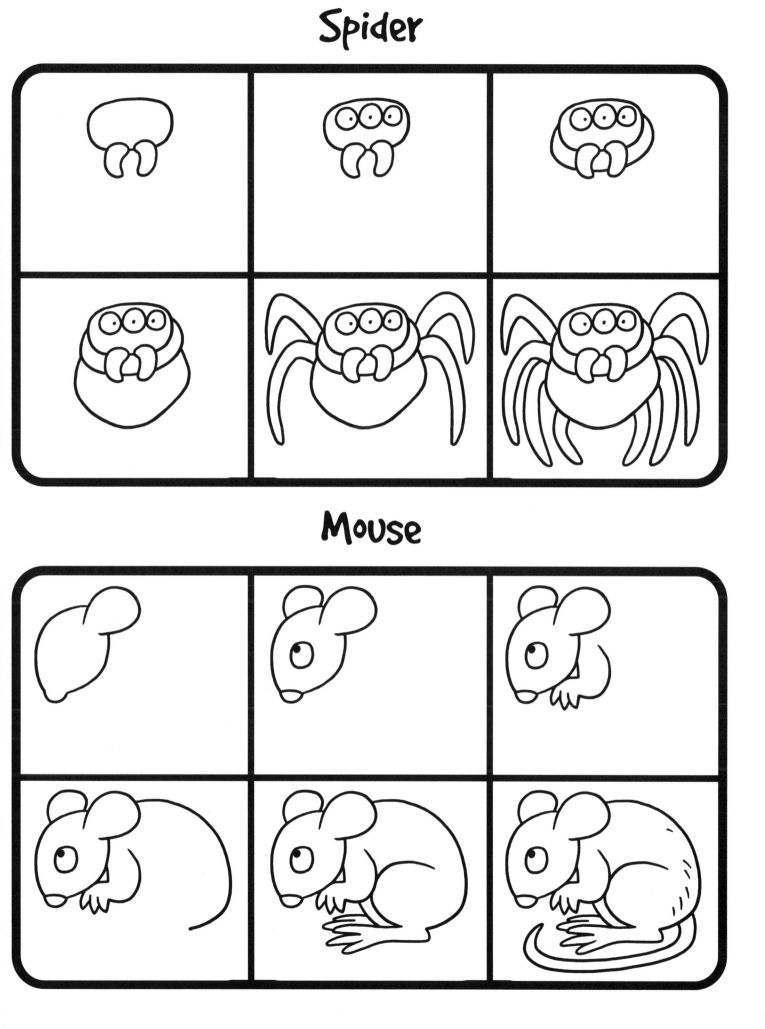

Mouse

Flamingo

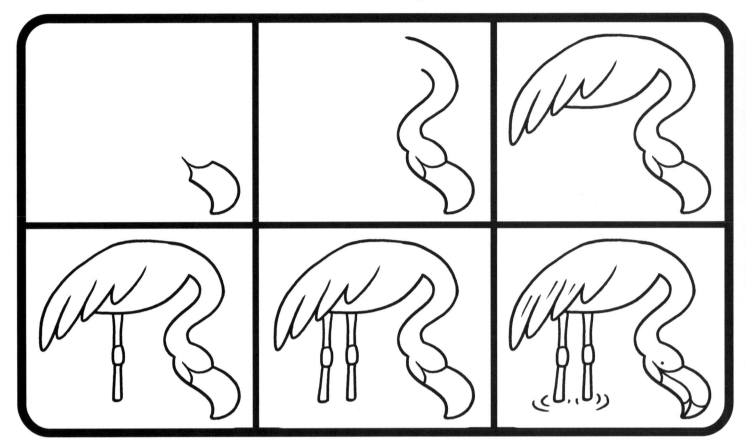

Bear

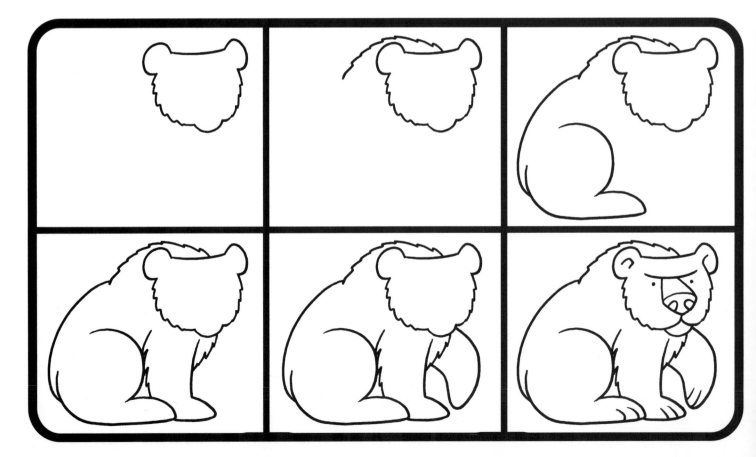

Sloth

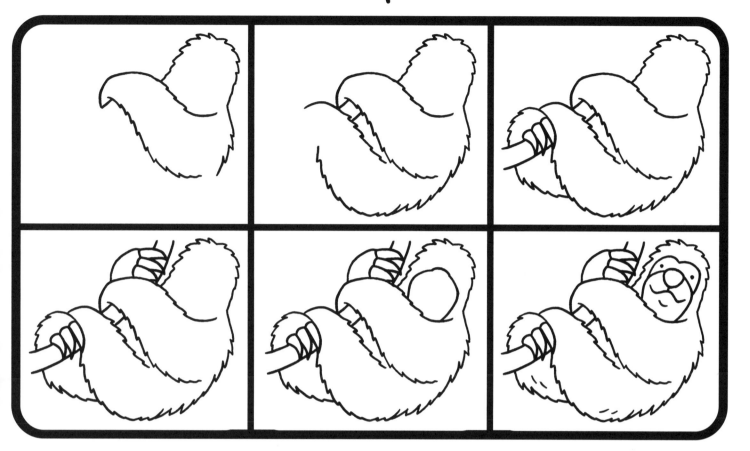

Hippo

Buffalo

Dragonfly

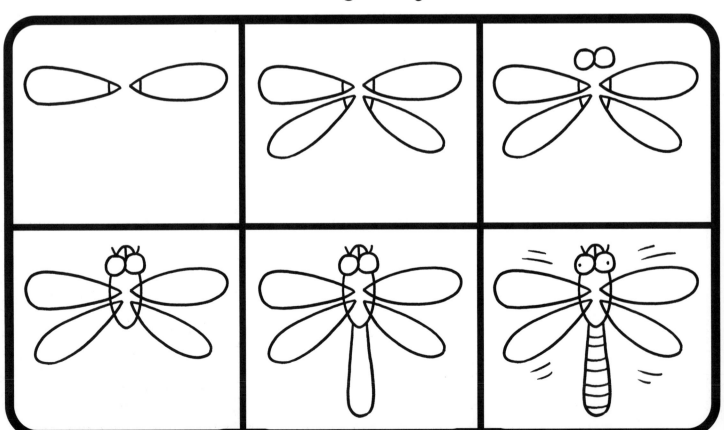

cheetah

Shrimp

Monkey

Heron

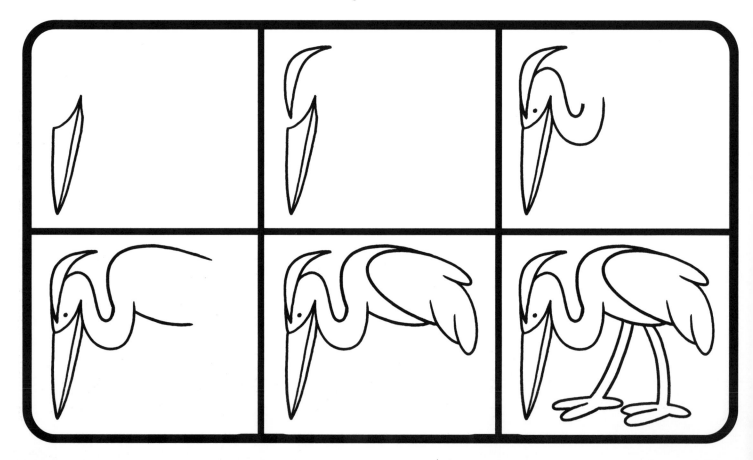

Puffin

Armadillo

Octopus

Bee

ostrich

Gorilla

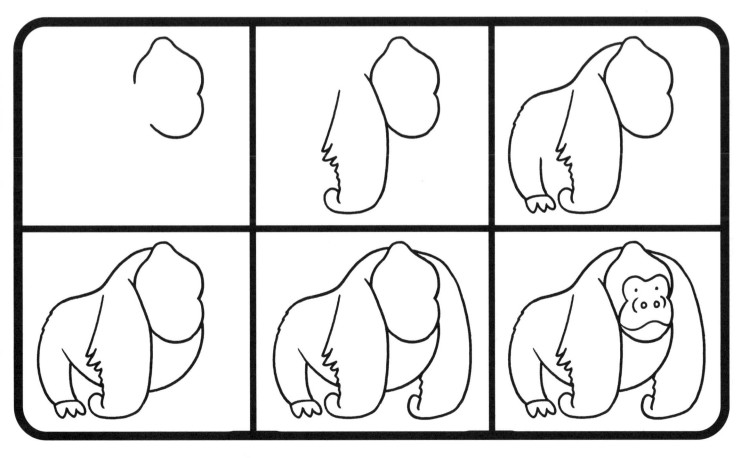

cuttlefish

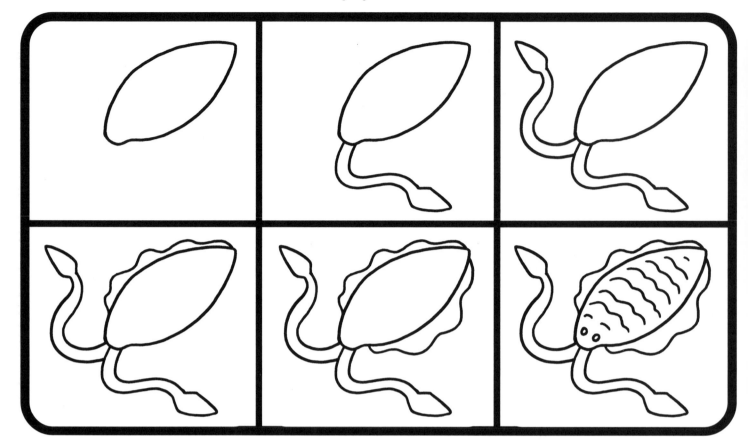

Ladybug

Swan

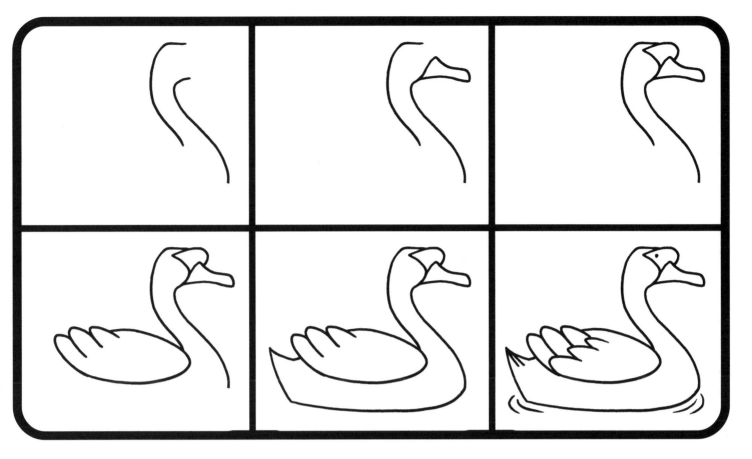

Manta Ray

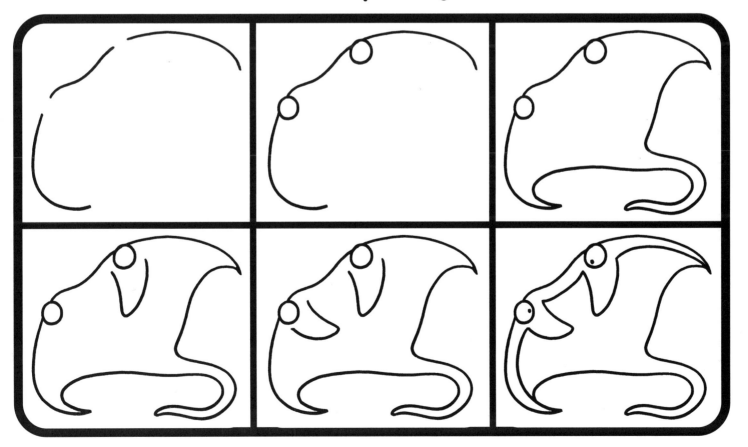

Blue Whale

Crocodile

Worm

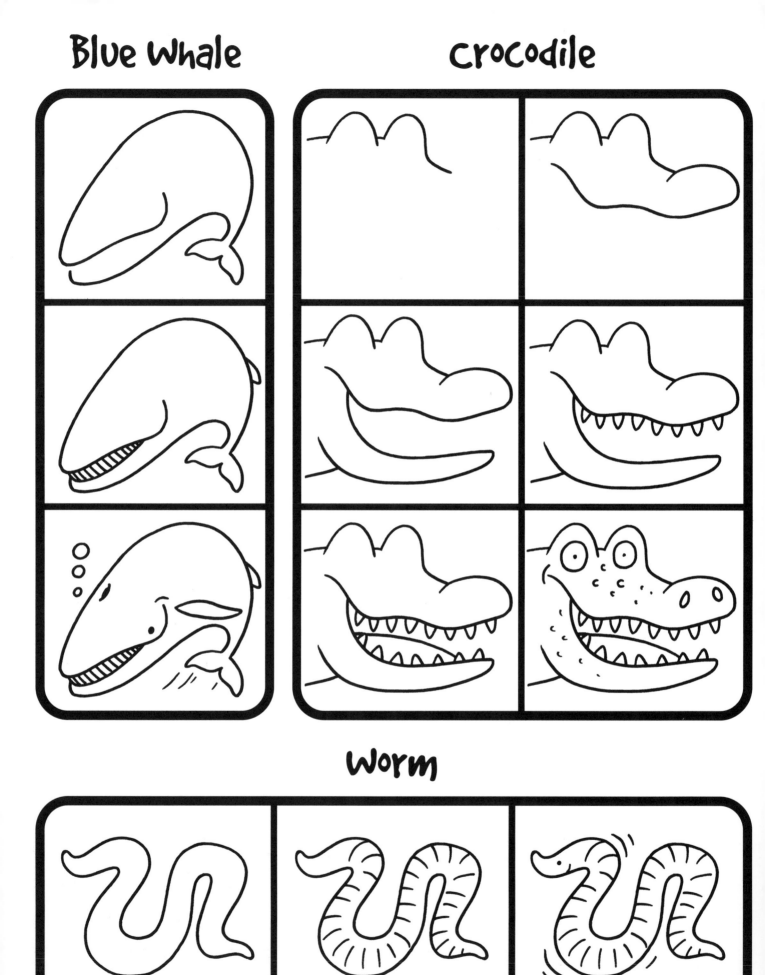

Wolf

Mole

Angler Fish

Starfish

Polar Bear

Hammerhead Shark

House Fly

Woodpecker

Sperm Whale

Angel fish

Cobra

Butterfly

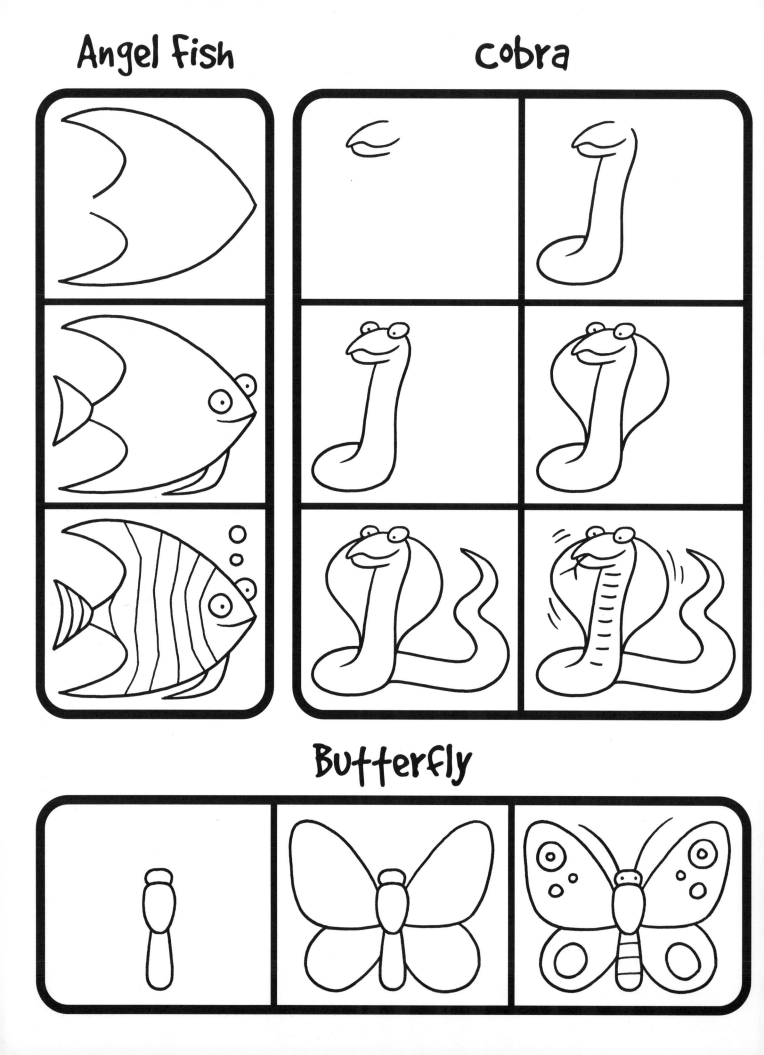

Tortoise

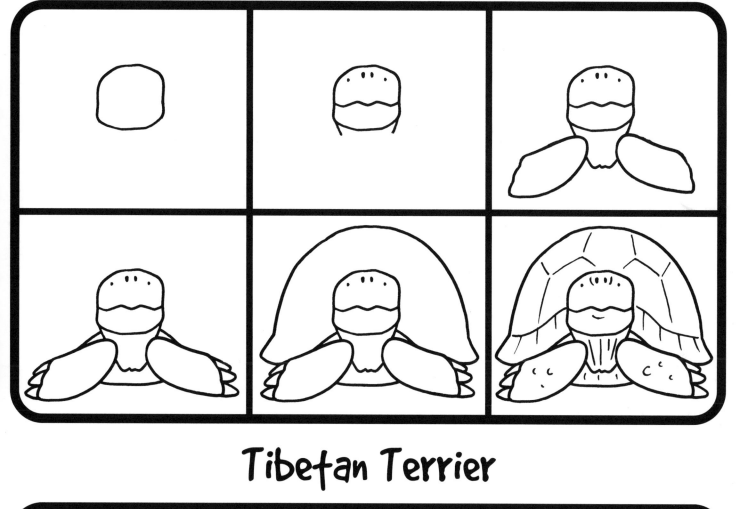

Tibetan Terrier

Peruvian Guinea Pig

Monkey

Poodle

Praying Mantis

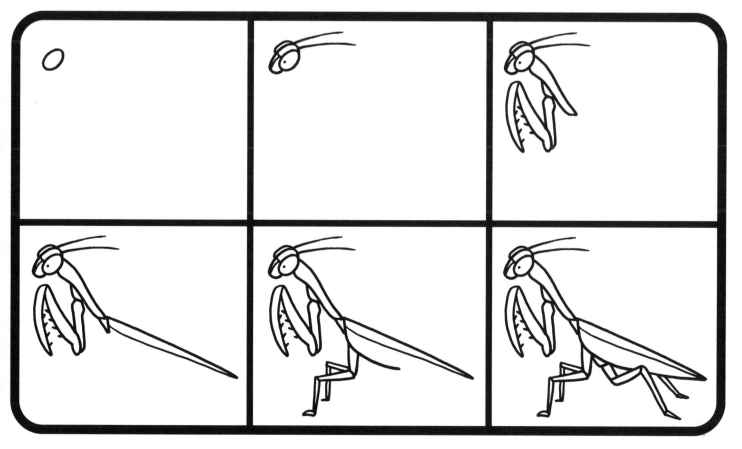

Puppy

Dachshund

Moggy

Abyssinian Guinea Pig

Rex Rabbit

Tree Frog

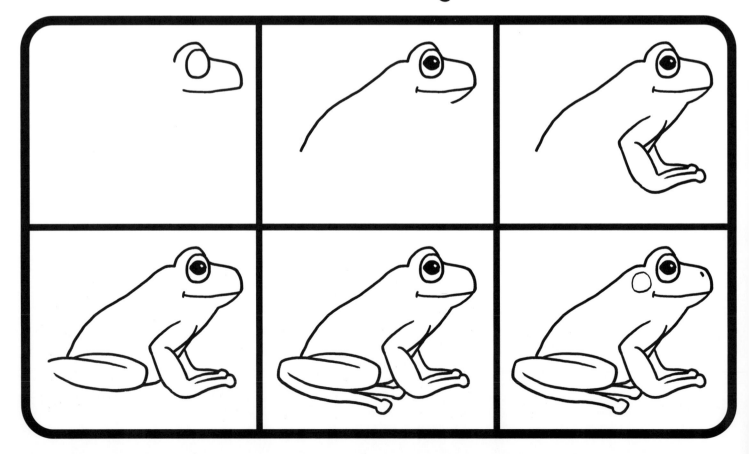

Lhasa Apso

Axolotl

White Mouse

Persian cat

Siamese cat

Lop Eared Rabbit

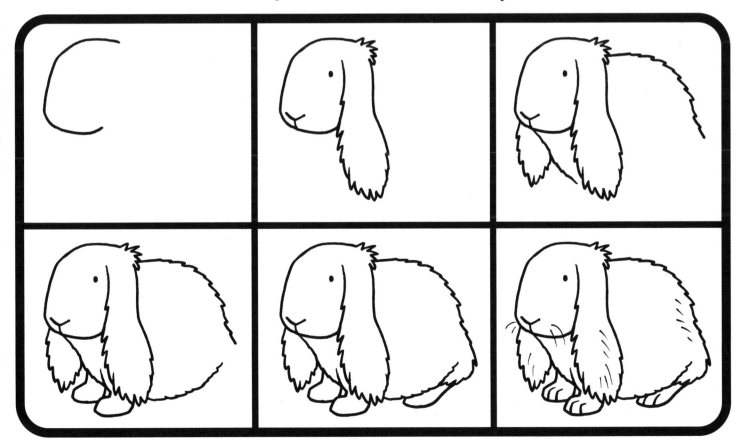

Python

Kitten

Rat

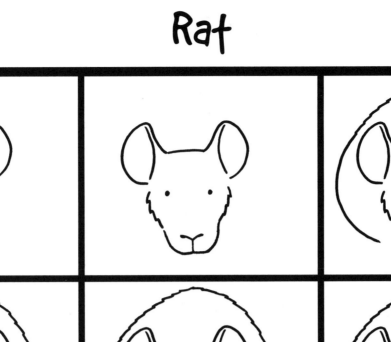

Beagle

Sea Monkey

Netherland Dwarf Rabbit

Giant African Snail

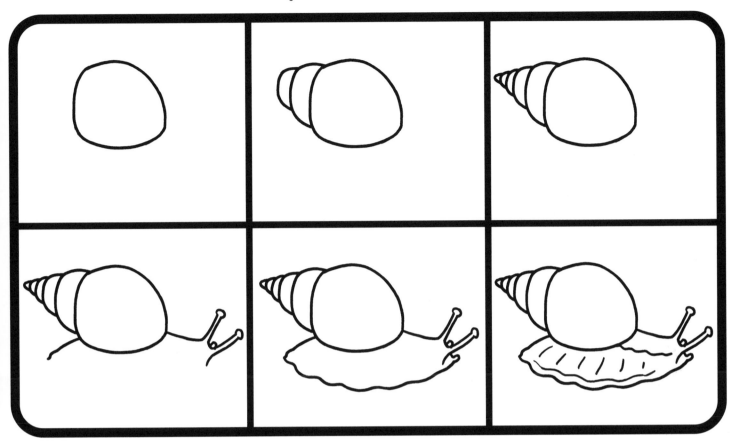

Springer Spaniel

Baby Rabbit

Angel Fish

Great Dane

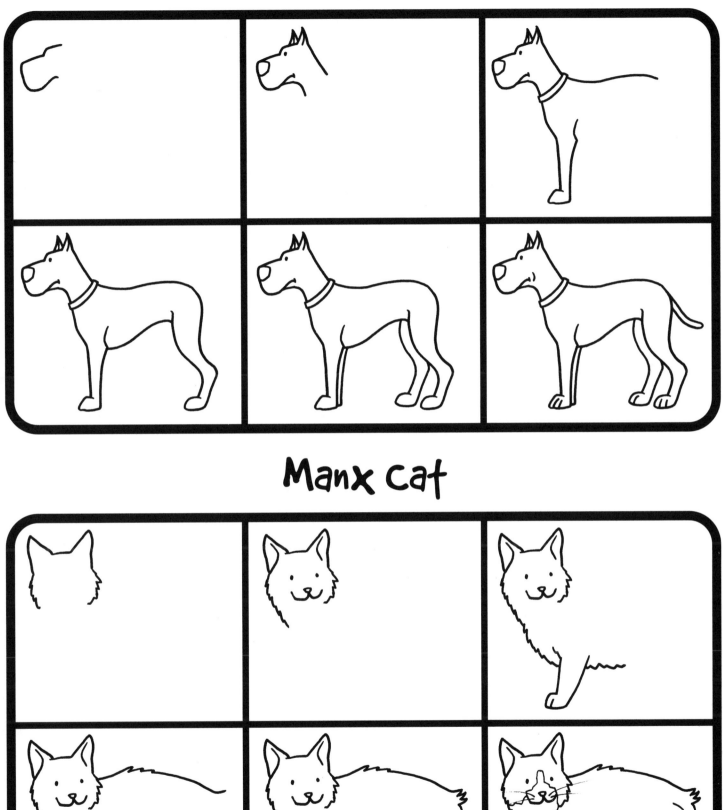

Manx Cat

Dwarf Lop Eared Rabbit

Bichon Frisé

Donkey

Saint Bernard

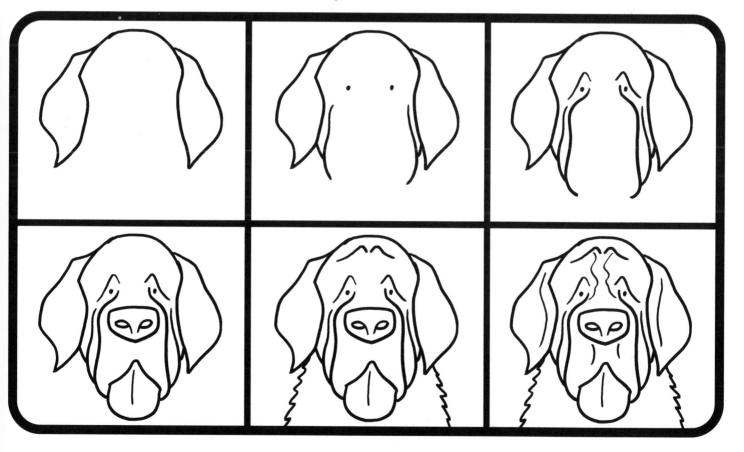

Pot-bellied Pig

Parrot

Boxer

Chameleon

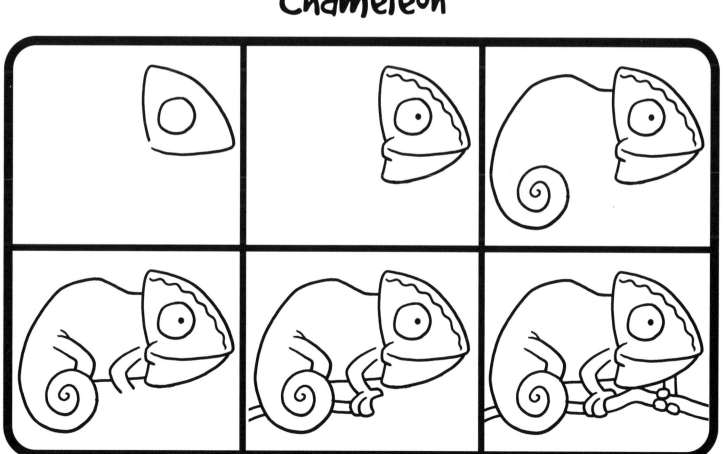

Siamese fighting fish

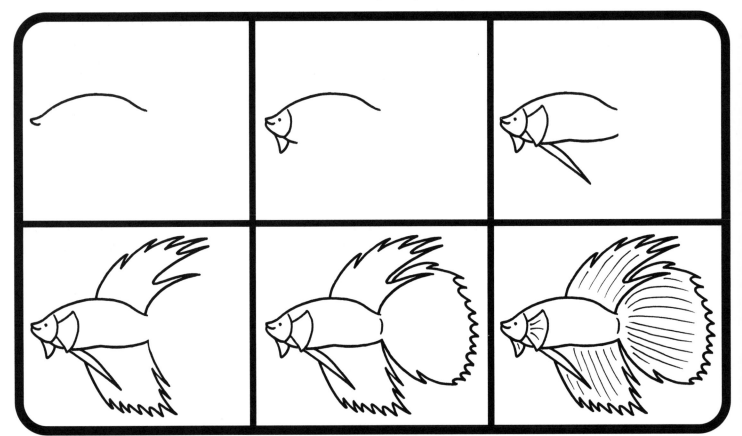

Newt

Chinchilla

Pug

Budgie

Bulldog

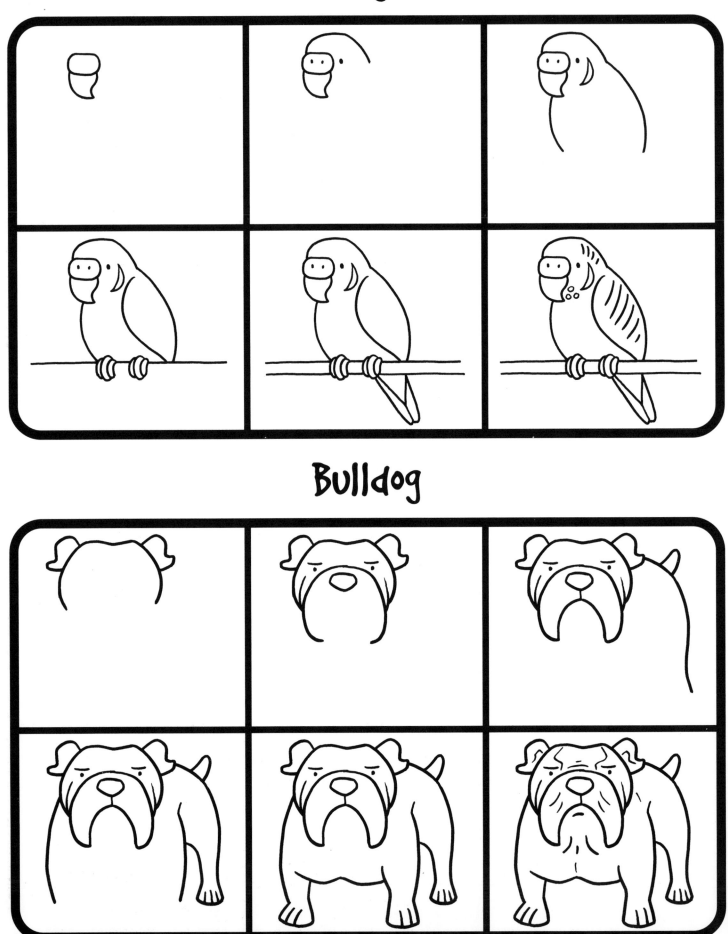

Milk Snake

Pigeon

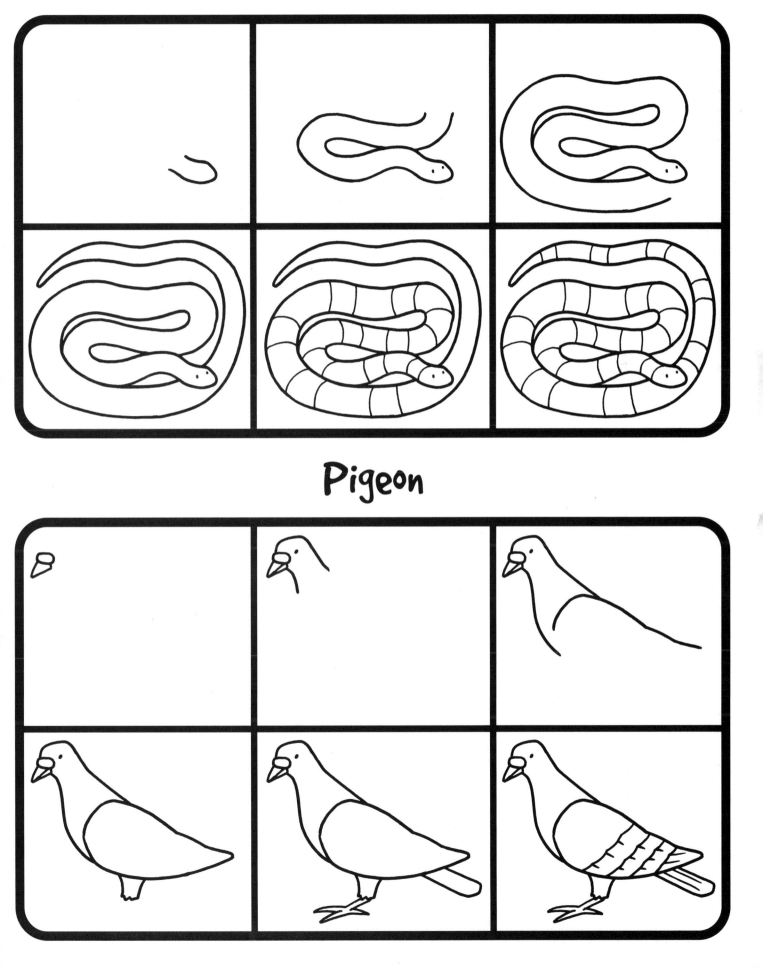

cockatoo

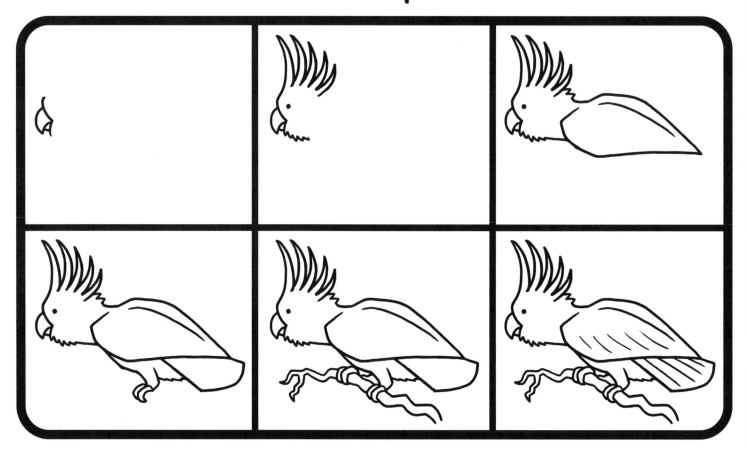

Goldfish

Long-haired Hamster

Piranha

cockatiel

Salamander

Stick Insect

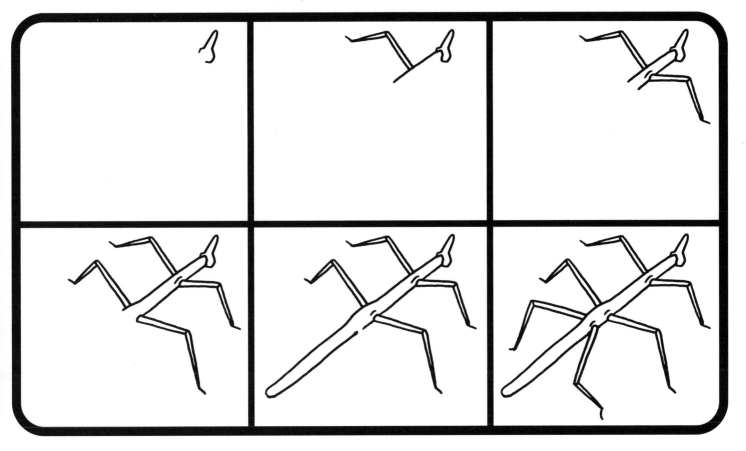

Mynah Bird

Canary

Gecko

Dalmatian

Short-haired Hamster

Catfish

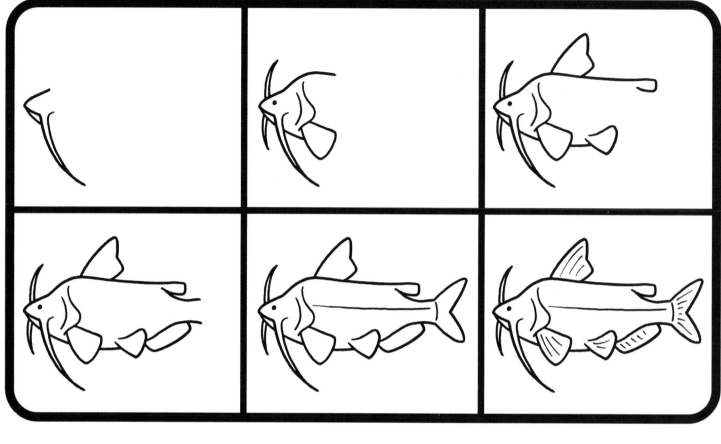

Labrador

Gerbil

Hermit crab

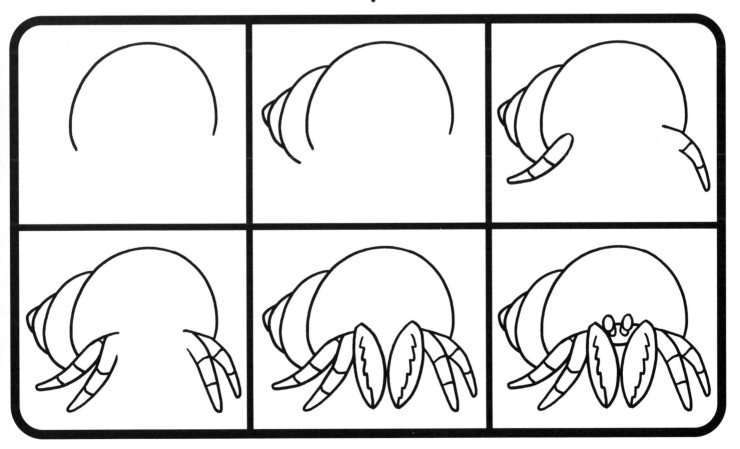

Golden Retriever

Ant

Maine coon Cat

Russian Hamster

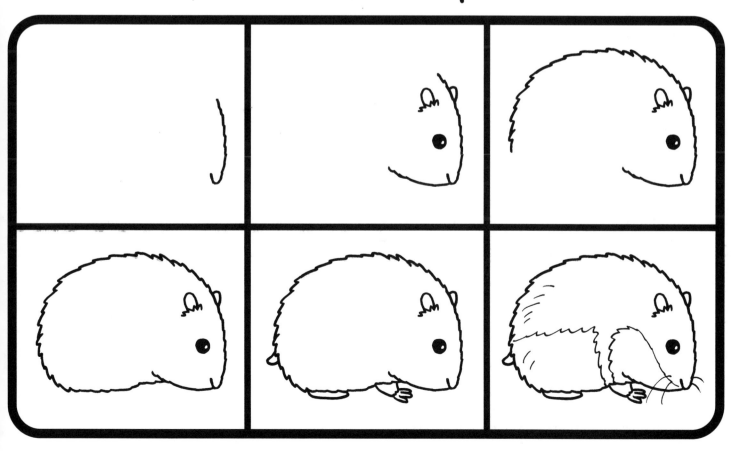

American Short Hair Cat

Bearded Dragon

Samoyed

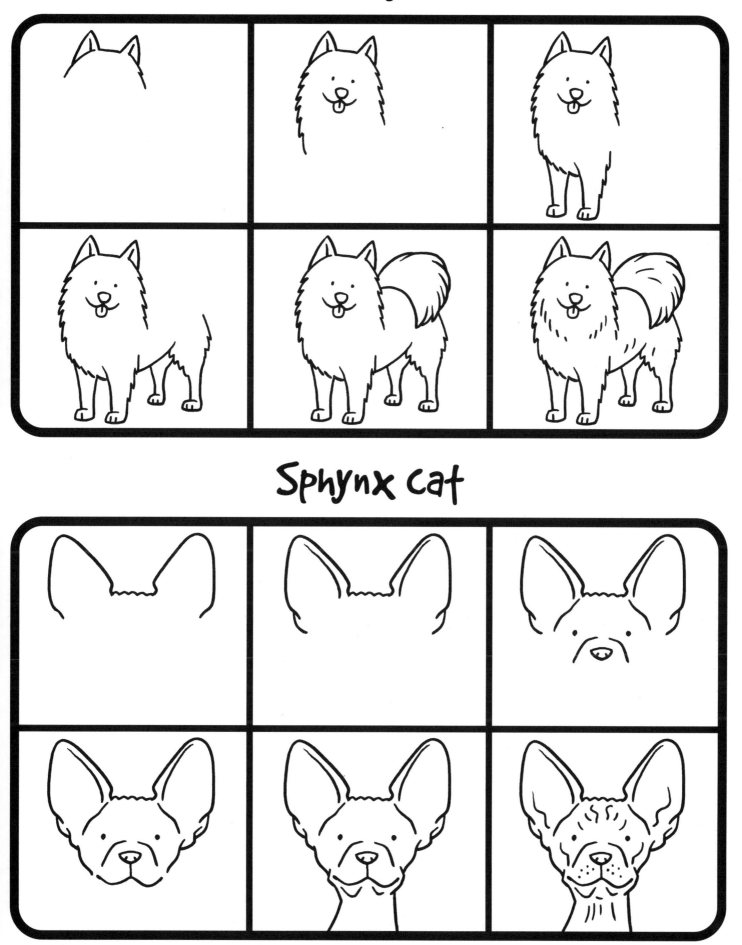

Sphynx Cat

old English Sheepdog

Tarantula

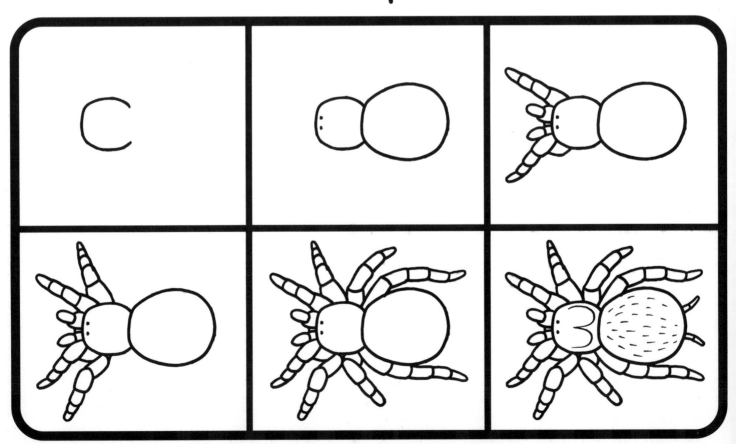

Hamster on wheel

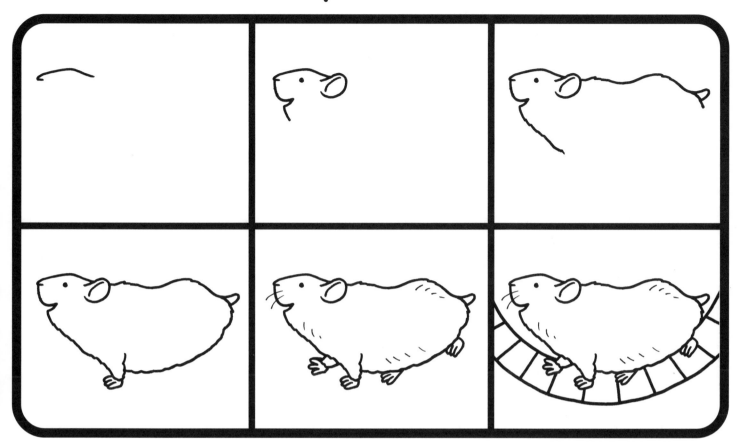

Chicken

Iguana

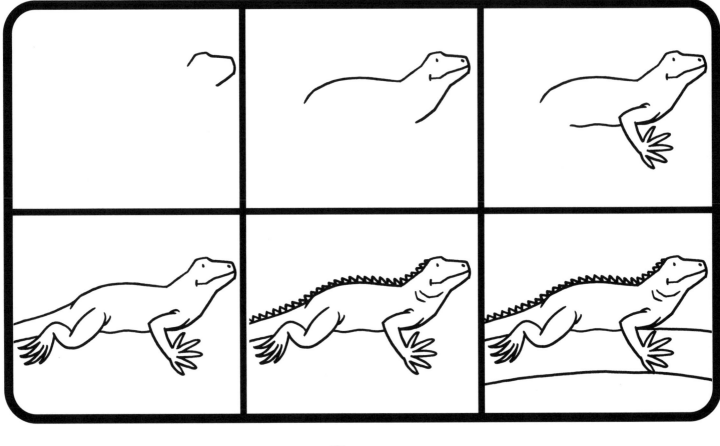

Frog

Egyptian Mau

Terrapin

Goat

Basset Hound

Chipmunk

Burmese Cat

Giant Millipede

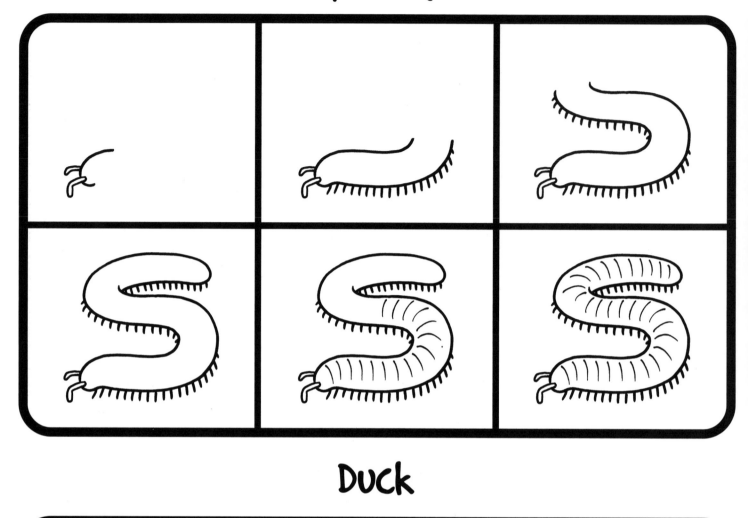

Duck

Abyssinian cat

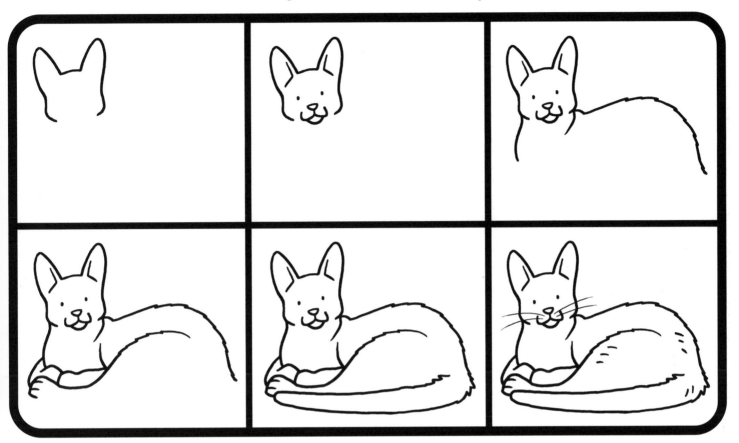

Hungarian Puli

Yorkie

Ferret

Scorpion

Alsatian

Birman Cat

Shetland Pony

Clownfish

Chihuahua

Angora Rabbit

Guinea Pig

Bengal cat

Lovebirds

Ragdoll cat

Chinchilla cat

Water Dragon

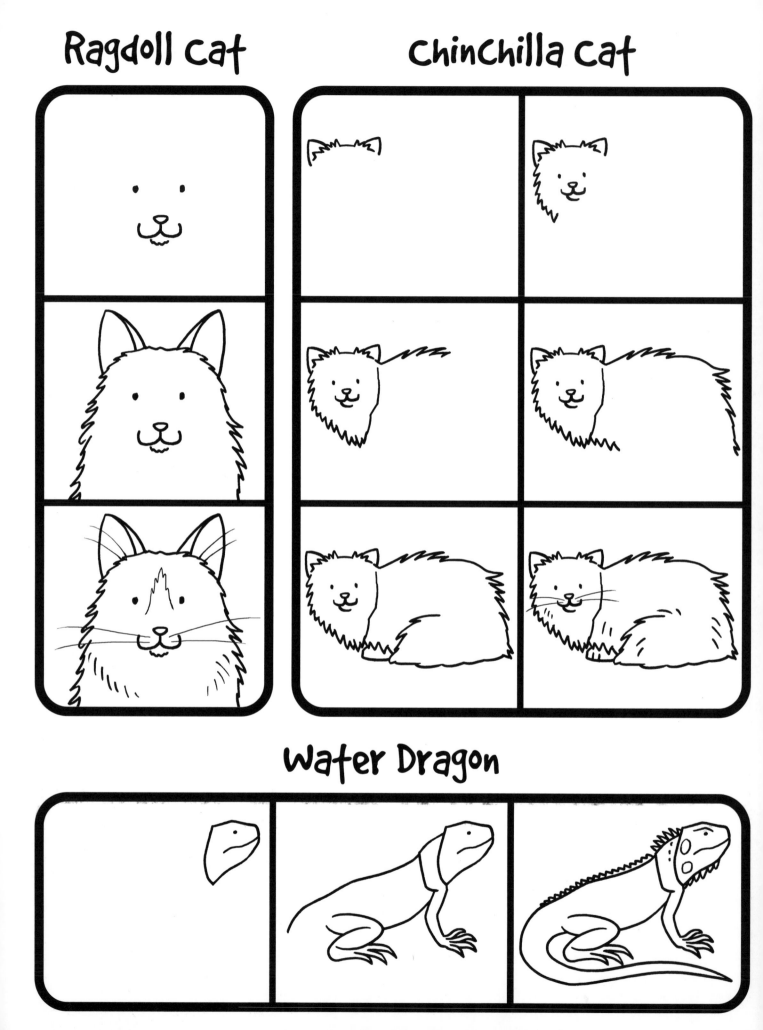

Roman Soldier

Baby

Roller Blades   Mechanic

Astronaut

School Girl

King   Queen

Doctor

African Musician

Mom   Dad

Brother   Sister

Gran   Grandad

Pharaoh   Clown

Skateboarder   Greek Scholar

Cowboy

Flamenco Dancer

Toddler   Judge

Greek Soldier

Victorian Lady

Teddy Boy   Teacher

Black Belt   # Sailor

Tennis Player

Builder

Bride

Santa claus

Roman Emperor

Nurse

opera Singer   Sheriff

Artist　Witch

Dentist

Soccer Player

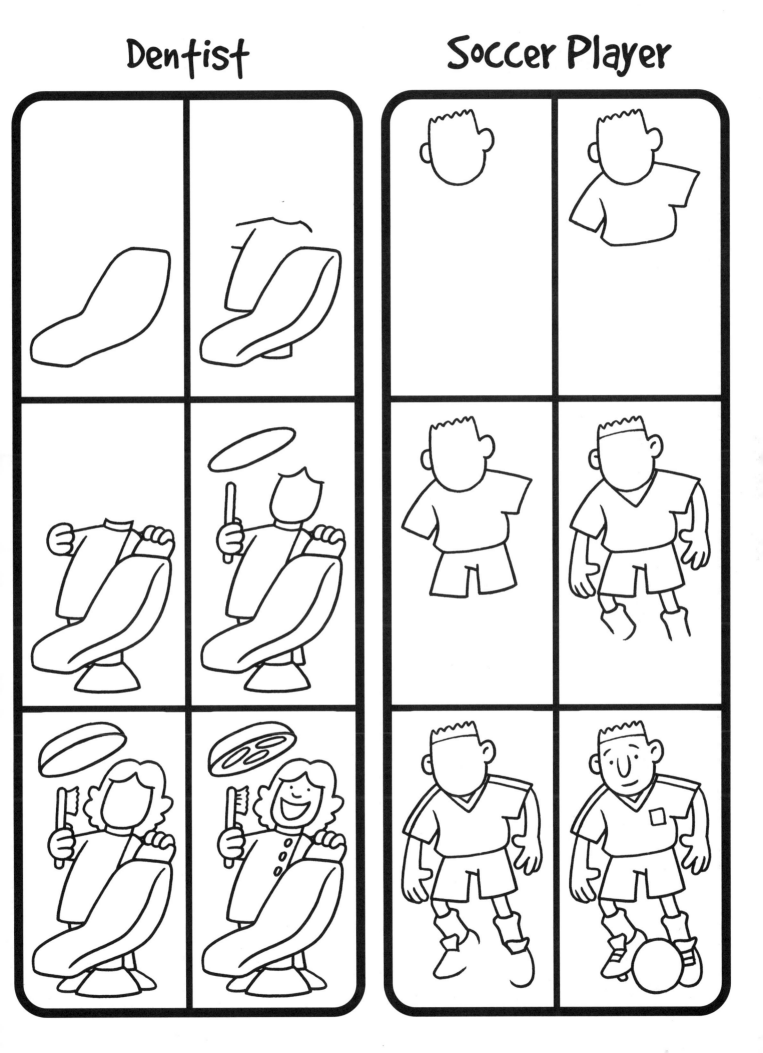

Ice Skater

Superhero

Diver

Burglar

Chef   Elf

Cave Woman   Cave Man

Gardener

Baseball Player

Fairy

Baker

Tightrope Walker   Fisherman

Magician   # Knight

Policeman

BMX

Rock'n'Roll Dancer

Mailman

Inuit

Scuba Diver

Fireman

Arab

Hippy

Lumberjack

Emperor

Indian Dancer

Victorian Gentleman   # Ballet Dancer

Painter

Farmer

Viking   Jump

Skip

1970s Pop Star

Actor

Handstand

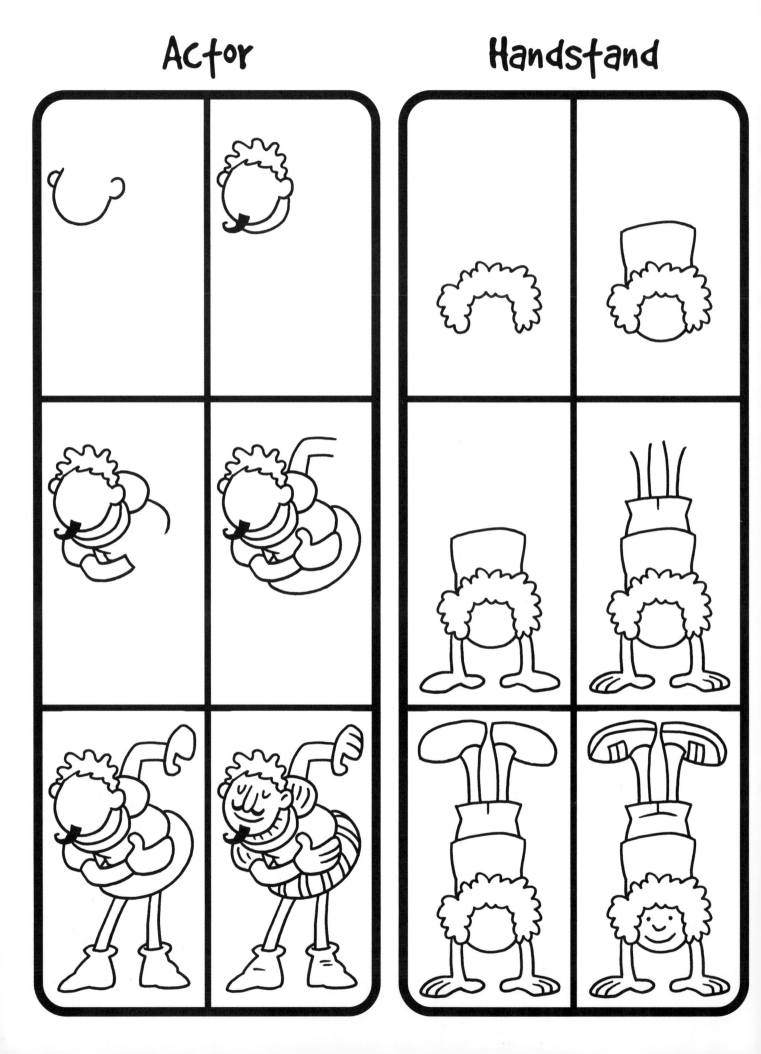

Surgeon

Chinese Lady

Scientist   Butcher

Pirate   # Mountaineer

Deep Sea Diver

Wizard

Captain

Dwarf

Tarzan

Skier

Surfer

Vicar

High Jumper

Weightlifter

Juggler

Conductor

Basketball Player

Waiter

football Player